The Dark

Poetry by James Harpur

A VISION OF COMETS
THE MONK'S DREAM
ORACLE BONES

Translation
FORTUNE'S PRISONER
The Poems of Boethius's Consolation of Philosophy

James Harpur

The Dark Age

Anvil Press Poetry

Published in 2007
by Anvil Press Poetry Ltd
Neptune House 70 Royal Hill London SE10 8RF
www.anvilpresspoetry.com

This book is published with financial assistance
from Arts Council England

Designed and set in Monotype Bembo by Anvil
Printed and bound in England
by Cromwell Press, Trowbridge, Wiltshire

ISBN 978 0 85646 404 1

A catalogue record for this book
is available from the British Library

CONTENTS

'And ween not, for I call it a darkness or a cloud, that it be any cloud congealed of the humours that flee in the air, nor yet any darkness such as is in thine house on nights when the candle is out.'

CLOUD OF UNKNOWING, Chapter 4

'We pray that we may come into this Darkness which is beyond light, and, without seeing and without knowing, to see and to know that which is above vision and knowledge.'

DIONYSIUS THE AREOPAGITE,
Mystical Theology, 2

ACKNOWLEDGEMENTS

Poems in this collection have previously been published or accepted for publication in the following periodicals: *Agenda, Cork Literary Review, HQ, The Irish Times, London Magazine, Magma, Oxford Magazine, PN Review, Poetry Ireland Review, Scintilla, The SHOp, Southword, The Stinging Fly* and *Stride*. 'The Monastic Star-Timetable' won first prize in the Scintilla Short Poem Competition 2003; 'Alien' won second prize in the Peterloo Poets Competition 2005; 'Stroke' won second prize in the Féile Filíochta Competition 2005; 'On Reaching Buddhahood' won second prize in the Manchester Cathedral Competition, 2003; sonnets from 'The Dark Age' sequence were shortlisted for the Listowel Short Poem Prize 2005 and 2006, and for the Féile Filíochta Prize 2005. 'Scribe B' and 'Verbum' are extracts from a poem commissioned by the Poetry Society as part of their Poetry Places scheme. 'James' is from *The Gospel of Joseph of Arimathea*, published by Wild Goose. 'In Prison', 'Nero' and 'The View from Heaven' are from *Fortune's Prisoner*, my translations of Boethius's poems from *The Consolation of Philosophy*.

I would like to thank Peter and Kit as usual for their excellent midwifery; Anna Adams, Alyson Hallett, Rosemary Canavan, and Ian Wild for their helpful insights and encouragement; Pat Cotter of the Munster Literature Centre for all his support; and Ian McDonagh and Cork Arts for a generous bursary that helped me to finish the book; and Evie and Grace.

Part One

On Reaching Buddhahood

ROSCOMMON RAIN

When the rain stopped the rain began
And clattered beads of runny light against the panes
Decreased and crept inside the ghosts of sheep
And seeped inside the warmth of prostrate cows.
Then pelted bogs to syrupy peat
Made gravelly lanes glitter again
Beneath the melting greys of cloud and cloud
Pierced the puddles with a thousand stings
Tumbled silver through the hedges
And off the skinned shin-bones of trees;
Swept, soft again, like a haze of locusts
Across the ridge, then shifted shape in sudden wind
Drifting, finer than chimney smoke,
Like a passing pang of some great loss
Away from where more rain was coming in
From somewhere else beyond the world's rim
Erasing gradually the misconception
That the world had ever not been rain
And rain would cease before the end of time.

STROKE

I   DOCTOR

'Afraid it looks as if she's had a stroke'
He says, quite calm, as if it were the flu.
There is an emptiness beneath her look.

I stare, I will, I pray, attempting to revoke
His sentence, so reasonably intoned. But no,
'Afraid it looks as if she's had a stroke'

Plunges like a needle. I fight the shock.
He asks her what my name is. She doesn't know.
There is an emptiness beneath her look.

I watch her consciousness drift off like smoke.
She dribbles into one-way sleep. *Don't go.*
Don't go. '… it looks as if she's had a stroke'

Keeps whispering – we wait and count the clock
Against the ambulance – so bloody slow!
There is an emptiness beneath her look.

At last the night's a blue-pulsed stroboscope.
She leaves the house, the world perhaps. I'm so
Afraid, afraid she's had a stroke
And of that emptiness beneath her look.

II HOSPITAL

There was a replica of her in bed
Behind the curtain – a good facsimile,
Surreal, not quite alive, and not quite dead

It seemed; a changeling, the real her spirited
Away into the world of memory.
There was a replica of her in bed

Sitting up, usual breakfast pose, her head
Tilted to read the paper with her tea
Surreal, not quite alive, and not quite dead

Her face pale white and hair too neatly brushed,
Eyelids at rest upon eternity.
There was a replica of her in bed –

The waxy tableau, sleeplessness, now made
Me feel disjointed, numb – I met her half-way
Surreal, not quite alive, and not quite dead

In limbo at the crossroads of two worlds
Before we moved, on different trajectories.
There was a replica of her in bed
Surreal, not quite alive, and not quite dead.

III HOUSE

The spirit of the house had been set free
Sundered like soul from flesh to leave a shell,
An undistinguished vacancy.

Windows were nerveless eyes that could not see
And every jumbled room an empty cell.
The spirit of the house had been set free

Threads dripped from her unfinished tapestry.
Dust filmed the mirrors; everywhere you could smell
Nothingness, an undistinguished vacancy

In her wardrobe, slippers, bed and diary
Whose space foretold a void none could foretell.
The spirit of the house had been set free –

We felt like squatters, pinched, temporary,
Acclimatizing to the spell of neutral
And the undistinguished vacancy

Drifting through kitchen, lounge, conservatory
As if it were a boarded-up hotel.
The spirit of the house had been set free,
Had left an undistinguished vacancy.

O'DONOVAN, O'DONOVAN, O'REILLY AND ME

At a time of terrorist alert
We clicked off headlights by the guardpost
Handed in our names and waited
Then revved the car, lit up its eyes,
And drove between façades of dormant barracks
Until the British airbase rolled apart
Like an international airport
Extinguished by a power cut.

The runway's black expanse of asphalt
Gathered speed from giant hangars
Towards the boundary of night
And seemed so desolate, wind-swept,
As if it needed something out of space
To come down from the clouds
And spark its braids of landing lights.

In the Mess it was another world.
We four aliens corralled ourselves among
The glazy crooners wailing like the dumb
To music blazing into engine roar.
A giddy couple shuffled out a pirouette
In the shadows of the dance floor.
While drowning in conversation
And matching meanings to the fish-lipped words
I tried to keep my eyes from lighting up
Whenever I glanced your way.

Outside again, the glared city clouds
Flew parallel above the sleeping runway.
We taxied cautiously from the car park
And forked right at the Spitfire:
One false turn would have brought us into
The immenseness of the landing zone.

In the shrinking hours of night
We welcomed home your lamplit street
And snug half-timbered terraced house
And while the others slunk upstairs
You led me out to show me your small garden,
The patch where you had cleared the weeds
And would wait for grass to prick the surface.

The tangerine clouds had gone,
Winds had shocked the grime from outer space
And sparkling like mica the constellations
As if rejoicing at an imminent arrival
Had switched on every landing light
In avenues of stars across the sky.

ALIEN

for Grace

My soul, there is a country
Far beyond the stars …
HENRY VAUGHAN

There: a planet full of seas and craters
Its mists of light and shadows detailed by
This photo printed on a scrap of paper.

A more than middle-aged astronomer
I scan this map for signs of life … and look!
Emerging from the grey – an alien creature

A small unearthly being, here, arrived,
The *thing* I feared would end my life, the thing
My mother would have died for, had she lived.

Dear soul, did you pick up the fuzzy thoughts
We sent as hopeful signals into space
In search of life and track them to their source?

Now you've landed, I feel the pang of age –
The undimmed glow of drawn-out childhood days
When growing older seemed like a mirage.

Now time is just an issue of dismay:
I pretend I'm one year older than I am
To quarantine each eager fresh-faced birthday.

I'm sad as well because I'll never know,
Probably not, the ending of your story.
What happened when I left? What did you do?

Have children in the sweet release of pressure?
And show them photos of your not-yet parents
Evolving in school line-ups to the future?

Did you shake off my shyness, hermit ways,
And curse an absent God and pointless life
And wonder why we brought you to this place?

Dear little traveller, may you forgive
Ancestral faults and ones we made our own:
Remember that we sent for you in love.

May you adapt and breathe the oxygen
Of this new world, pick up the signs and codes,
Human disguises, masks I tried to learn.

Be blessed to find a kindred alien –
Watch out for eyes, and smiles, and chance remarks
In crowds or somewhere lonely like a mountain

And maybe in the future, the stars uncurtained
On a summer's night you'll show the one you love
The shining home you lost, where I've returned.

ON REACHING BUDDHAHOOD

I'd longed for it for years: the holy hush,
Desires retreating in the harvest moon –
An open eye stilling the jungle crush

Of fronds, birds, ferns, the insects of ideas –
The creeping quiet, as after a monsoon,
The blessèd emptying of hopes and fears

The drying trickles of anxiety
Nirvana opening like Gautama's smile
A slice of moon beneath the bodhi tree.

Instead, I find I've gained the Buddha's belly,
And I meditate, cross-legged, on lust and bile
Or watch, serene, the *maya* of the telly

Forgetting if I can the looking glass
And Buddha's balding pate, unholy arse.

Part Two

The Dark Age

BRENDAN

The naked hermit, cliffs of ice, the cold,
The island of the saints emerging from
Black fog as light, its shore of powdered gold

And apples ripening in every orchard
The youth who welcomed each of us by name –
These died around the settled fires of Clonfert.

But Judas on his rock, wind-burnt, stripped wise,
Writhing above the slaughter of the sea
Remains pristine inside my deepest darkness

His eyes alert for the approach of demons –
I see them glowing as when we rowed away
And hear his voice above the raucous ocean,

'Hell is stasis, keep heading for the sun
And when you reach the light, sail on, sail on.'

PATRICK'S RETURN

I sensed at once the yearning for release.
March mists dispelled the coloured countryside
And hung in curdled webs from ragged trees.

Soft rain soaked fields of stationary bulls
Where gangs of crows were cackling like the druids
Who came to curse me, clacking jaws of skulls.

I sensed the people crying out in sin;
The eyes of severed heads still globed their hell
Of blood and fire, gluttony and drink.

My prayers were sucked from me and overnight
God's love descended like a snowfall.
The blackthorns opened up their petalled light

And everywhere I tapped my staff, my wand,
The fields and trees leapt up to green the land.

CANAIR IN THE AFTERLIFE

We needed one another for salvation
But Senan didn't know that, shrieked and wept
When I rowed out to his island in the Shannon,
And he wild haired, half nude, all dirty –
He would have thrown me to the tide except
He was too pure to touch a woman's body.

In time my love woke his, his deepened mine.
We peeled each other's hearts to innocence:
Naked to God, we shone like seraphim.

And now I see my bones as white as any man's
Below the golden soil and smile content
At Senan's daily softening grief, like Adam's

When he remembered Eve returning through
The dusk, oblivious of the creeping shadow.

CIARAN DISCOVERS CLONMACNOISE

On Inishmore I saw the mystic tree
Grow huge before me: branches, twigs unfurled
A globe of shimmering capillaries –
Wide-eyed I watched the thickening fuzz-green light,
The lengthening shadow – birds that swooped and whirled
Returning to their distant homes with fruits.

I quested day and night to find that tree
Until one day while resting by the Shannon
Watching its waters filing through the reeds
I felt it there inside – a surge of joy
Took root, my body grew, my heart expanding

And thrust up to the sky I saw below

The world grow dim and pilgrims from afar
Converge in lines of light to form a star.

COLUMBANUS'S JOURNEY

My ancient body cried for peace, for death,
As we raised our tents beside the alpine lake.
That night an angel came and shrunk the earth
Before my eyes: one small part glowed, but most
Was pagan dark – what could I do but take
My staff and plod towards the mountain snows?

I wept when we arrived at Bobbio –
I knew it was the end and felt as free
Beside that fish-lit stream as long ago
When leaving home I'd tried to reassure
My flailing mother, who slapped me, hugged my knees
Then rolled across to block the open door

And I had sprung screaming past her body
Knowing that leap would be my longest journey.

COLUMBA'S EXILE

A place where Ireland is invisible –
The verdict was the lodestar of my will
Drawing along the foaming coracle

For I knew I'd be distracted from the Lord
If my heart's eye from every cliff or hill
Migrated back to Derry, Donegal.

Then landfall on that sunny grainy day –
Iona, fireflies of drizzle, *tabula rasa*!

But Satan must have been a stowaway.

I drowned myself in books and catching fish,
In songs and fasts but still the dreams increased,
My soul reviving what my mind had crushed:

Unable to see home the more I saw
The hounding fields of Derry, Donegal.

GOBNAIT'S END

Nine pure white deer would mark my bed of earth,
The angel said, and my rising into glory
But not on Inishmore.
                              Afraid of death
Wondering what devilish trick could blanch deer
I left to flee the ending of my story,
Those bloodless creatures sucking on my fear.

I tried to slip my fate in woods, strange valleys.
I chanted, prayed to slow my heart, but still
I heard the pulsing of mortality.

Until that snowing day near Ballyvourney.
I almost missed them standing by the hill.
White against white
                    nine curls of breath.
                                        The journey

Stopped. I kneeled. Thanked God. Shook off the fright.
Then rose up in the glow of falling light.

KEVIN AND THE BLACKBIRD

I never looked, but felt the spiky feet
Prickling my outstretched hand. I braced my bones,
My heart glowed from the settling feathered heat

And later from the laying of the eggs
Heavy, as smooth and round as river-rolled stones,
Warm as the sun that eased my back and legs.

When I heard the cheepings, felt the rising nest
Of wings, the sudden space, the cool air flow
Across my fingers, I did not know the test

Had just begun – I could not bend my arms
But stood there stiff, as helpless as a scarecrow,
Another prayer hatching in my palms –

Love pinned me fast, and I could not resist:
Her ghostly nails were driven through each wrist.

KIERAN OF SAIGHIR AND
THE HARPISTS

Weird it was! the mirror of the lake, the tree
Jiggling light: eight silver harps were spiked
On it, their strings caressed by twigs and leaves.

I prayed, and prayed, until the waters shrank
And eight white corpses loomed like great long pike.
We took them out and laid them on the bank.

Again God blessed us, and death twitched into life:
Their eyes unglued, flicked madly at the day –
They stood and stretched, we struggled with belief
As haloed with a flowing watery light
They fetched their harps and then began to play
Such sweet songs freshly brought from paradise

We wondered whether it was we who'd died,
Were being welcomed to the other side.

ST CARTHAGE IN THE MONASTIC GRAVEYARD

That evening the sun was slanting out the crosses
When time expanded, nerves of colours woke
Deepening the green of leaves with grass and mosses ...

And then I saw it move, I swear, the soil moved –
A face emerged, moon-white, rose slowly, spoke:

'We live here so alone, cut off from love.
For Christ's sake bless us so that we may rise
From this no-man's-land of separation –
Lead us, together, into paradise.'

My heart knotted as I told him he must wait
In darkness till the final resurrection;

And still I see his face sinking to the fate
That haunts my sleep, where scratching dreams express
My daily boxing in of loneliness.

ENDA AND THE BRIDE OF CHRIST

I hoped the rolling sea of Inishmore
Would mush the memories of her convent,
Her face, her body, on the marbled shore;
That my kneeling naked, impotent, in caves
Would freeze my lusting for her innocence
And cool my psalm-mumbling lips that crave
To whisper in her hair, caress her forehead,
To kiss the pale shells of her eyelids
Cupping her sight towards the eunuch dead.

I pray with outstretched arms until they're numb
I pray until the sense breaks into bits
And then I pray to Christ to make me dumb
Before I scream a curse to drown the wind,
Dying for my sweet bride who married Him.

FURSEY'S VISION

The Anglian fens flow tide-like from my door
The sky is yellowy grey, builds up the snow,
And oaks explode in tangled lightning forks.
Watching the rain become harsh sleet

I see a midnight valley
                              fiery glow
Demons dragging a sinner from the heat
Blistered puffy lips
                              dead-fish eyes;
I knew that wretch was me
                                        his clasp and kiss
Seared on my flesh
                              my lust, envy, lies.

My penance? To be a *stupor mundi*
Rehearse my tale, reviving the abyss,
Parade my scars and sweat for all and sundry,
Pilgrims who seek the furnace in my cell,
Inside my eyes, two trapdoors into hell.

FINTAN OF CLONENAGH

The soldiers brought their trophy heads to us –
Great swinging bulbs, onion-bruised, purpley,
The thin lips shrunk around the final rictus.
We bathed and dabbed them dry as honoured guests
Then dug out grave beds in the cemetery
And, like mothers, laid them lovingly to rest.

Lord, can any life survive these nameless heads?
At what point does our flesh succumb to death
For good – what if we'd buried just their teeth instead?
Can prayers conjure souls from claggy clay?

We need imagination, Lord, not faith,
To see their bodies on the final day
Grown whole again from spirit-watered seeds
Breaking the earth as carelessly as weeds.

Part Three

The Monastic Star-Timetable

JAMES

from 'The Gospel of Joseph of Arimathea'

The tiny window fed mosquitoes
Into the room. I won't forget
The steady chewing of bread
Intrusive sniffing, gulps of wine,
Each conversation stifled by
The airlessness that it created;
And I remember wondering why
I felt no love for anyone.
He looked as if he hadn't slept
His hair fell down like stringy seaweed
His words were too familiar –
I could have mouthed them as he spoke.
He said we had to stay together
To face the coming dangers.
Right then I wasn't bothered whether
We did or not. I didn't care.
We seemed to be well-meaning strangers
Making the best of it because
We knew we wouldn't meet again.
And then he blessed each one of us
In turn. And no one said a word.

Morose, we left that room late on –
So wonderful to breathe the night –
Followed him through the eastern gate
And stumbled up the gloomy slope
Past outcrops and the arms of trees
That loomed like crosses on Golgotha.
Behind, the temple was a mountain,

Rising against the starry heaven
And streaked by whispering shadows
From countless torches, passing lamps.
And suddenly I felt at one
With everything, with life itself,
Connected with the past and future –
I felt so proud to be a Jew
To hear the singing from the tents
To be a part of this great feast
With Moses looking down on us
And all the kings and prophets too.

He led the three of us away
To a small clearing in the trees,
I was reminded of the time
When he became a torch of light
Up on that mountain in the north,
With angels on his right and left.
Those were the figures I saw
While drifting into sleep, the earth
So welcoming, and pilgrim songs
Mingling in the scented darkness –
Next thing I hear the blurted grunts
Of someone yelling in a nightmare.
I scramble up and see him crouching,
Talking to Peter, or was it John?
And then the thuds of padding feet
Torches moving through the trees
And shouts as if from stricken animals –
The eyes of Satan everywhere –
I don't know what I'm doing, then
My arms are wrenched behind my back
And someone hits my head – the world

Distorts, cracks into sparks,
Hysteria, and voices crying
So loud they would have raised the dead
As if the trees, now come alive,
Are screaming like the dying.

ST SYMEON STYLITES

I

Heat struck,
Horizons wobble with clarified smoke.
The desert is a sea-bed
From which all water has been burnt.
Creation, here, was impotent
Except in sand, rock,
Spikes of grass, and head lice.
A sweep of mountains, heat glazed,
Cuts off this adamantine paradise
From profanities of the vulgar.

I have all day to turn
Towards the compass points
In rhythm with the sun
And watch the emptiness besiege me,
Advancing sand that never seems to move,
An army of nothingness

Melting away to nothing with the night.
I am the centre of a cosmos
Lit only by my eyes.
I am the sundial of the Lord:
My shadow is the time
He casts from eternity.

I used to have this dream at night:
I'm in a desert digging
Like a scorpion escaping heat;
The hole becomes so wide and deep
That I'm enclosed, as if inside a well,
And lightly touched by cooling shade.
Each spade of sand expels a sin
Relieves the pressure on my soul
And lights my body from within
But makes me see more dark below.
And so I keep on digging
Until I wake and grasp the light of day.

In time I came to realize
The dream was upside-down:
I built a mirror hole
But made material with blocks of stone.
Here, on top, I rule myself,
My palace a balustraded stage
Its roof a canopy of endless blue,
My hunting grounds a sea of dust.
I hear no voice except my own,
Exclaiming curses, prayers – if only
To remind itself of sound,
Or whispering in my head, where I revive
The chatterings of Antioch

Damascus and Jerusalem,
Of hermits gossiping in mountains.

Lord, is it heresy to think
That isolation smoothes the path to you,
That people are infectiously corrupt
Trampling silence, stillness, solitude
In their scramble to relieve
The agony of imperfection?
When I was earthbound, a penitent
Chained up on a mountain ledge
I could not pray except to pray
For night to be protracted
Against the wave of dawn that broke
Against the rock, unveiling shepherd boys
Foul-mouthed, throwing stones,
And ragtag pilgrims
Drifting from oracle to oracle
Led on and on by questions
They kept unanswered
To give their lives a meaning
Their legs some exercise.

Forgive me Lord –
I think I hate my neighbour.
I may be of the world
But now at least I do not touch its surface.
I know I hate myself,
Fearful of life's contaminating fingers,
Dreading the day's effluvia
That slip through each unguarded sense
To rot inside my head;
More and more I'm cowardly

Afraid of love's attachments
Afraid of death's infinity
Afraid of sleep, darkness, demons
Scuttling, their eyes as grey as stone.
I know I have to make myself
Into a desert, a vessel scoured,
For you to pour your love in me
And turn my flesh to light.
Instead at night foul dreams
Fill me with women I once knew –
But slightly rearranged and naked –
Who dance through veils of sleep
Whispering to my virginity.

It's said that like draws like.
How putrid I must be inside
That I'm forever feasting on
Anger, lust, spite from years ago
Recalling in excruciating detail
Unwitting slights that pricked my pride,
And letting vengeance grow
With such grotesque intensity
The bile would poison all the Persian army.

Most days I think I'm split in two.
A spirit yearning for the light,
And a body of delinquent appetites
I tame by standing stiff all day,
Watching its scraggy silhouette
Revolve around me slowly
Waiting for hesitation, weakness.
I set my will against my flesh
But when the sun is swallowed up

I join the dark, become a shade
Within the filthy anarchy of dreams:
Helpless, adrift, I'm turned nightlong
Around the memory column of my sins.

At dawn I wake, bursting to feel the joy
Of Noah floating free towards
A shining uncontaminated world.
But when the sun erupts
I am a tatty raven in a nest
Of sand, hair, albino faeces
And bread rinds a half-wit monk
Lobs up to me with water-skins –
A wingless creature dreaming of flight
Feeling the desert cram inside me
Every loneliness I've ever known.

The desert's fields of nothing
Are giant mirrors of my soul
Reflecting every scrap of sin;
The more I purge myself
The more the specks crawl out
Like ants I stamp to death in rage –
How can God love my shrinking flesh,
My frailty, lack of constancy?
Why does he wait to strike me down?
I bow a thousand times a day –
At night I stay awake to pray
And pray to stay awake.
Sometimes I wonder if I pray
To keep the Lord away?

2

I bow a thousand times a day
Until my will's a reflex
The blinking of an eyelid
My body supple as a snake.
I feel the clot of pride dissolve
And anger, fantasies of sex
Flow out until I'm empty.
And yet some nub of me remains,
A grit of self impeding me from God.
What else can I do?
I know I must excise my 'me'
To make the space for God to enter –
Yet who but I can do the surgery?

I pray for grace to fall like dew
But all that comes to me is dew.
I seek God in the sky all day,
He hides behind the sun's white mask;
I scrutinise the desert
Deeper and deeper; but nothing moves
Except a spray of sand
The lazy wind occasionally shifts.
I scan the night and walk along
The stepping stones of stars
That lead across the black abyss –
But I get lost in the immensity.
There is no-one to lead me
There are no arms to hold me
No hands to wipe away my tears.
Am I untouchable?

It is my will that makes me pray;
Yes, I confess, not love, but will
Honed sharp by discipline,
A spearpoint piercing frost and sun:
To think about, anticipate
The benediction of the cooling dusk
In the middle of the day
Just for a second
Would break
The spell that ritual repetition casts
And tip me over into madness.
I must keep vigil; and if the sun burns out
My charity and tenderness,
It is the price I have to pay
To keep my will intact.

What is it, Lord, obstructing you?
I drive my will to drive my flesh
But no amount of will, it seems,
Can drive me to your embrace.
So how much higher must I climb
To see you, or even just the angels?
I doubled this pillar's height
To glimpse your blinding glory
To catch the singing of the blessed
And all I hear is the wind
Sighing and groaning like a crippled beggar;
And all I see is sand, dull sand,
Spreading towards a haze of greyish white
And rocks much smaller than before.

What sin remains in me?
Was it humility I left behind on earth?

I take no chances:
I starve myself to kill my pride
I stand until my knees rebel
And buckle in my tuberous legs –
The pain becomes a balm,
Soothing the sense of being damned,
A hell in which the recollection
Of the slightest misdemeanour
Feels like I've crucified a man.
Lord, I've made my head a skull
Of lizards, my heart a stone.
Soften me, give me another sign.
I would have, I admit, renounced
This life but for your crumb of peace,
One moment in two thousand days.
Memory kills
Whatever it revives, but still
I conjure up this bliss of consolation:

One morning in late spring
I am distracted by a shadow wheeling
Around my feet, a bird above me
Shifting from height to height
And gliding round and round
Unwinding in its smooth ascent
The cord that's twisted round my soul.
I feel my spirit lift and lighten
My thoughts suspended
In the evolving silence.
Although the sun is overhead
The desert is so softly coloured
And distant hills are brighter:
Everything appears benign –

The jagged rocks, wisps of cloud,
Grass, particles of sand vibrate
Released from boundaries of form,
Distinct and somehow joined
As if the light between them has intensified
Has drawn them into unity
Like a sea surrounding islands.
And I am part of this enchantment.
My sense of self has been unravelled
And only joy remains
At my arrival
In the land of milk and honey.
I feel like singing to the Lord;
Instead I thank him for this grace.
I have to think with care
To choose the words.

And that is my mistake.

3

Crowds scar
The blank and beautiful horizon.
They come in dribs and drabs,
Shuffling, rough, some yelling from afar –
As if my memory has cracked apart
Releasing all the wrongs I've done
From the beginning of my life
To press and heckle me
To plead for resolution.

They camp around my eyrie
Shaded by hides or wicker frames,

Yabbering anecdotes, taking bets,
Or shouting up their prayers and names,
Or turning spits of rabbit, goat and lamb.
But I am higher than before.
I rise above them like a hoisted sail
Free from the tentacles of arms
And opened shouting hands.

At night the desert merges with the sky
All dark and calm and smooth
Unrolling to infinity.
The campfires dim;
I know this is the perfect time
To bring my feelings to a centre
Recollect my thoughts
And be a silence for the Lord to enter.
But I am paralysed, alert,
Waiting for yawns, coughs and spitting,
The creaking of the ladder
The first determined face
A basket's offering of bread and water
And sickly letters of petition.

Lord, give me back my solitude.
Grant me peace; grant my soul peace.
Surely it cannot be your will
That I should preach, releasing
Your word in ripple after ripple,
While all the time my spirit
Vertiginous with anger
And rigid as my spine, condemns
Their stale intrusive lives?

They come from Rome, Constantinople,
Like rats to a rubbish heap
To watch me pray – to watch me crack? –
Half monk, half entertainer
A scrawny bird with bulbous ribs
Prostrating like a demoniac
Sun-burnt, wind-burnt, frost-burnt,
A freakish act that they've created.

I may have made them come to me
But they have helped to make me what I am
And not what I would be or do:
To sing the psalms at break of day
My spirit rising with the sun
Inching towards your stillness, unstained light.
Instead I smell the odour of their sins
As pungent as their roasting meat.
I pray for them by day, by night,
I pray to cleanse their copulating minds
To cure their rabid neediness
And so I exorcise my hate for them
My hate for me.

Lord, protect me from the One
Who tempts me into hate, and pride,
Just as you did not long ago
When Sirius lay above the mountains.
That morning, I heard the ladder creak:
Another busybody or petitioner –
Another prayer aborted.
A man arrived, red-faced and sticky
A tiny girl strapped to his back
Her face consumed by leprosy.

I stopped prostrating, helped him up,
He held her out, tried to speak
And stammered, 'a gift from God'.
I snorted.
Then took her, muttered pieties
And quickly traced a cross
On her forehead, neck and nape.
But as I made to hand her back
The man knelt down and bowed
As if I were a king.
I don't know what possessed me.
I held her high above my head,
An offering to God –
How could I anticipate
The frenzied cheering of the crowd
The chants of 'Symeon, Symeon'
Louder and louder round the column?
How could I guess the pumping thrill,
The sudden ecstasy
From the power of my kingdom?

That night a bluish glow descended
As if the moon was shining on
My platform and nowhere else.
The light was alive, intelligent –
It seemed to concentrate in front of me
And draw me in: I did not move
But let myself become enfolded –
I felt I was suspended in the air
Weightless, cleansed of thought.
Then the shock, light flared
A crashing of a mighty waterfall –
A chariot of fiery bronze burst

Towards me like a sheet of flame.
I clenched my eyes, looked
Between the slats of fingers
And saw an angel with pale skin,
A smiling female face
Beckoning me towards the chariot.
I thought my time had come at last,
Reward for all my bitter loyalty.
I placed a foot inside, pushed down
To step on board but stumbled, turned
My ankle, fell and cried to God –
Just then another angel
Appeared from nowhere, chanting,
Holding up a golden cross –
The first was drained of light,
Its face turned grey and scabby –
I swivelled, tried to run
But could not move, a searing wind
Burnt my neck, back and legs
As the chariot roared off through the night.

Next day I cracked my body like a whip
To drive out all satanic pride.
Two thousand times or more I bowed
Refusing water, bread and pilgrims.
I nearly died. My hips were two hot pins.
In time I warmed to this regime –
Besides, what other course was open?
Constrained by debilitating sins
The narrowing of my spirit
Too near to earth, too far from heaven,
I could only drive myself to ecstasy,
Or build a higher column.

4

The sky falls upward as before
The crowds are gathered as before
The desert still sweeps out towards the mountains
But everything is different
Because my eyes see through another heart.

I stand inside the centre of myself
A pillar of stillness
Unable to be interrupted
Because there is no me to interrupt.
There is no me but Christ
And Christ is not disturbed.

The metamorphosis occurred
A year or so ago
When I was bowing to the Lord
Resisting heat and nausea:
My ulcerous leg sprang out,
I crashed down flat. Stunned
I staggered up and tried to bow again
But dropped and smashed
My temple on the balustrade.
I must have lain for hours –
The hottest time of day
And everything had gone to sleep.
I could feel the moisture leaving me
My brain turning like a spit.
I prayed but nothing came
Except the drumming of the sun.
I listened to the buzzing in my ears –
Was this susurrating hum of dying? –

A cloud oozed up behind my eyes
A cloud no prayer could pierce.
I lay there listening to my heart
And to my inward voice reciting
Endless rounds of praise
My will was powerless to stop.
A shell enclosing darkness,
Enclosed by darkness,
A thinning consciousness
Listening to itself listening
I clung on until the final drop
Of self flaked off into the abyss,
And with the spiral of annihilation
The silence came
A flash
A blossoming of stillness
Removing me from flesh
Into the rapture of the dispossessed;
The wall of dark stayed dark
Constraining radiance
As if a sea of light was banked against it
And suddenly
I felt myself approaching God
Or God approaching me
The fibres of my being loosening
Opening, unfolding deeper
Beyond my will
Until a surge
Of joy, of love,
Flooded through me
Wave on wave on wave
And I was drowned
In the paralysis of light.

Bodiless, thoughtless,
Drifting to beautiful extinction
I heard a noise
As from another world,
The creaking of the ladder
Shocking me back to flesh again;
Then murmurings, a human voice,
Taste of water on my lips
A cloth laid gently on my head
The rhythm of cool air against my face.
Did I sleep for hours or days?

When I awoke I was not certain
Where I was; something was awry –
I lay too comfortably in shade
Beside a frame of woven twigs.
Fresh bread and water lay at hand.
I drank and ate, and drank, until revived
I clambered, rediscovered legs and feet –
Pain radiated like the sun,
My wound was crisp and puffy.

The day was drenched in clarity
The desert silent in its expectation.
And then I realized what was different:
The dread had passed.
My sense of sin had gone –
And my abhorrence of the world:
I knew I could descend
And that the ladder raising me to heaven
Was there to take me down to earth.
But there and then I chose to stay.
I felt at home at last.

And then I saw the crowd was watching me,
Waiting for words.
I did not have to think
Because I didn't have a thought.
I preached the word of God alright
But did not say a word
For there was nothing I could say.
Instead, without my willing it,
I bowed slowly to the west
Then south, east and north,
And as I turned to each direction
A wave of love flowed up to me
So tangible I could have jumped
And stayed afloat.

And now each day
I watch puffs of dust appear
The steady movement in the haze –
Peasants and emperors, the lame
On stretchers dragged by mules,
Astrologers and priests and monks
Merchants and soldiers, prostitutes –
Bearing the burden of their lives.

Each one of them is Christ
Walking alone through fields of wheat
Or by the sea of Galilee.

IN PRISON

I used to relish scribbling poetry.
But now I'm stuck with dirges born of sadness.
Look how the Muses, dishevelled by distress,
Prompt elegies that only make me cry.

At least they weren't put off by any fears
From being my companions on this journey.
They were the best thing of my salad days:
Now they console me in my sad last years.

A sudden spate of suffering and I'm old.
Decrepit from the tyrannous rule of anguish;
My hair's a snowdrift, prematurely white,
And flesh flaps off my clapped-out bones in folds.

Death's welcome when it passes by your prime
Arriving when you're begging for release.
But Death has turned a deaf ear to my prayers,
Won't close my red-rimmed eyes a final time.

When flighty Fortune brought me passing pleasure
I nearly came to grief at one dark point;
Now that her misty scheming face has changed,
My blasted life drags on at painful leisure.

Why did my friends harp on about my luck?
I stood on shaky ground: I came unstuck.

Boethius, *The Consolation of Philosophy*, I m. I

NERO

We know the havoc he wreaked: Rome blazing,
Senators cut down, his brother murdered,
And he, steeped in his mother's blood, appraising
Her corpse dry-eyed. Sizing up its beauty.

Boethius, *The Consolation of Philosophy*, 2 m.6: 1–7

THE VIEW FROM HEAVEN

*'The function of the wing is to take what is heavy
and raise it to the region above, where the gods dwell.'*
— PLATO

*'There is another life, emancipated, whose quality is
progression towards the higher realm ...'* — PLOTINUS

I have quick wings to fly you to the heavens
And when your nimble mind has put them on
It will despise the earth as something grim
And soar beyond the stretching realm of air
To see the clouds as tiny specks below.
Ascending through the upper realm of fire
That's heated by the ether's rapid movements
It rises to the starry Zodiac
To join the sun god's path or journey with
Cold Saturn or with coruscating Mars;
And where night glitters like a silver painting
It follows round the orbits of the stars.
Contented with its efforts up till now
It leaves the farthest limits of the sky
And stands upon the ether's outer boundary
Revelling in the awe-inspiring light.
For this is where the king of kings holds sway
Who holds the universe's reins and drives
Its speeding chariot – though he remains
Unmoved, the radiant lord of everything.

And if the path returns you to this place
Which you forgot but now attempt to find,
You'll say, 'This is my country, I remember!
From here I came – now here I've come to stay.'

And should you want to gaze down on the world
Of darkness that you left, you'll see as exiles
Those callous tyrants who inspired such fear.

Boethius, *The Consolation of Philosophy*, 4 m.1

SCRIBE B

My cell's a layer round my self.
I crave the light for copying
But everything light touches
Becomes one more distraction.
Outside, the bees and blackbirds,
Whitethorn, apple, hazel
Remind me of the life
I snuff to concentrate
On nibs and liquid soot.
My days are one long snuffing out:
Desire, envy, pleasure,
The memory of shrieking,
The impulse to expose
My personality –
Why is it such a sin
To be myself? God made me,
So surely what I am
Must finally come from him?
What point has self-denial
If God can't save his own?
I retreat. Shamed, I feel
The abbot's whispering words
Burning my cheeks:
'You are God's medium.
He does not want your thought,
Nor do you have to grasp
His every act or utterance
Revealed in history.
Your shaping of the letters

Into fully breathing words
The sound of vowel and consonant
The patterning of rhythm
Create the mystery;
They penetrate your soul
Despite your reason's protest.
Your bodies will decay
Your names will be unsung,
Your consolation is
Your blessèd anonymity
Commitment to a process
Where self is not inserted
Between truth and its expression.'

VERBUM

from 'Voices of the Book of Kells'

'Remember this: I do not have
A name or face, or form,
And words and paint prolong the lie
That I can be depicted: I am beyond
All sense of what 'beyond' can mean.
To know me you must close your eyes
And leave the road of affirmation,
The road of thinking and imagining:
Just be a pilgrim to yourself,
Alert, not knowing where to go,
But trusting in your ignorance
And travelling inward all the time.
Watch out for clues and signs – observe
The spirals of your thoughts,
The interlace of hopes and fears,
The circles of your good intentions
Revolving ineffectually,
The nibbling mice of jealousy
And hissing serpent of resentment –
Just watch your convoluting self
Proliferate without your intervening
Until it dies away to nothing
But silence and a glowing stillness,
As a stone exudes warm summer light;
And in that pregnant emptiness
You may just glimpse me
But only unexpectedly
Like a half glance at a sunshaft

Erupting in a neighbouring field;
And if you see me you've become
The unstained love you sought in me –
Then who is who?
The eyes through which you see are mine.'

THE MONASTIC STAR-TIMETABLE

'On the holy night of Christmas
When you see the Dragon above the dormitory
And Orion poised above the chapel roof
Prepare yourself to sound the bell.'

Darkness freezes round me in the cloister.
The vellum words and stars inflict their patterns
Whispering like the ceaseless prayers we send to God.
No one must lie asleep who must protect the world.

'On the festival of Saint Germanus
Look for the jewel of the Archer's arrow
Hanging above the middle of the tower:
That is when to start the night-time hymns.'

The stars are our seasons, the keys of our prison:
Winter snowfall, glittery scatterings of spring rain
The globes of poppies in the harvest fields
The dying meteors of copper beech, oak and elder.

'On the day of the Lord's circumcision
When the bright star in the knee of Artophilax
Is level with the corner of the dormitory
It is time to bring the taper to the lamps.'

The thrill of live flame! A writhing spirit,
The chapel like a soul skinned with gold.
This is the light I seek beyond the constellations;
O *lux aeterna*, burn off my crusted life!

'On the feast of our beloved Saint Agnes
When you see the Virgin's spears rising clear
Above the space between the sixth and seventh windows
Make ready for the sacred office.'

I dread nights of fog, mist, vapours, cloud
The clinging absence, the separation from God.
Lord, how long before a star expands inside me
Flooding my soul and flesh with gracious light?

'On the feast day of Saint Clement
Orion will rise above the end of the refectory –
But wait until you see the sword and scabbard
Before you wake the brethren.'

So many nights I've waited for eternity
Listening for music, looking for meaning,
But all I've felt is the dark between the stars,
My heart, beating like a bell, the phrases of mortality.

By James Harpur from Anvil

Oracle Bones

'James Harpur is not in the least like anyone else ... His is an amazingly consistent voice, compelling in its intensity. If you're brave enough, read him. He will take you into a world you will find difficult to forget.'

R. J. BAILEY, *Envoi*

'Harpur takes the stuff of superstition – a Celtic monk, a Delphic priest, an Assyrian extispicist, a superannuated auspex – and gives it a persuasively timeless, often disturbing significance ... *Oracle Bones* offers a kind of religious poetry. It does not, however, carry a whiff of the "pious" – rather, it has "a sense of the sacred running in parallel to the quotidian".'

PETER READING, *Times Literary Supplement*

'The volume of poetry published this year [2001] that I have returned to most often ...'

ANTHONY HAYNES, *The Tablet* (Books of the Year)

The Monk's Dream

'James Harpur's second book is disciplined, intelligent and repays several readings ... *The Monk's Dream* is an intricate exploration of death – not death alone, but the mystery that surrounds the experience ... In all, *The Monk's Dream* is a finely weighted and balanced work of elegy.'

RICHARD TYRELL, *Times Literary Supplement*

A Vision of Comets

'James Harpur's first collection [has] a sense of the sacred running in parallel to the quotidian, and while the poems often reach into the exotic or esoteric, they are nevertheless accurately and cleanly made observances of a world the senses have access to.'

MARY RYAN, *Poetry Ireland Review*

'Harpur's sensibility is attuned to love, time, myth, the numinous – the makings of poetry ... Harpur has an imaginative wonder.'

ANDREW WATERMAN, *London Magazine*